Civilian Lives Matter!

K. M. Patten

Civilian Lives Matter!

Other books by K. M. Patten

Tell Me Bad News
Indictments from the Convicted: Rants, Articles, Interviews and Essays
In Favor of Hatred
Staying ON During the Great Reset

Print ISBN 978-1-960405-45-6
ebook ISBN 978-1-960405-46-3

Cover Design by Guy D. Corp
www.GrafixCorp.com

STAIRWAY PRESS—APACHE JUNCTION

STAIRWAY≡PRESS

www.StairwayPress.com
1000 West Apache Trail
Suite 126
Apache Junction, AZ 85120 USA

Foreword, 2024

IF MY UNRELIABLE memory is correct, I began working on this essay sometime in 2014. Like the very people I take aim at inside these pages, I was motivated by outrage. Intersectionalists, Critical Race Theorists, and all Leftists of a social justice stripe have pushed a narrative that I think is incorrect. They maintain that the only people victimized by America's law enforcement are, and have been, black people.

More, that white people luminate with a kind of force field, blessed with the privilege of having light skin, and thus enjoying impunity from the police. Considering that I've been feuding with the police since my teenage years, I felt the need to explain how this narrative ran contrary to my own experience. Some of those encounters with the police have been noted here, and anyone is free to call me a liar or else do a background check.

As a misanthrope, "taking sides" is anathema to me. "Bothsideism" is sometimes seen as cowardly, but at least I never have to run defense for "my side" when it's revealed that they've done something horrible. "Yes, they're people, and people suck." Everyone is guilty of awful behavior. It only becomes slightly more upsetting if their actions turn out to be criminal.

Like all aspiring moralists, I'll rage about it, but only after a hard shrug. This should be expected of everyone and all "sides." Even MLK Jr. was said to be a serial adulterer and plagiarist. (Nevertheless, I still listen to his excellent "Beyond Vietnam" speech once a year.) Nobody is above criticism. Indeed, most are worthy of condemnation.

Bukowski once wrote, "the best at hate are those who preach love." Back when I first wrote this, Social Justice Warriors were often greeted with an equal amount of confusion and amusement. In the ensuing years, post-pandemic, and after the riots spawned by the murder of George Floyd (I, too, believe Derek Chauvin is guilty), it's even more obvious that many who rage against whiteness and police abuse have no problem wielding power and inflicting pain.

In my booklet about the Great Reset, I ask a simple question: How are we supposed to "defund the police" when we need the police to enforce lockdowns and vaccine mandates? I've yet to hear a good answer. Suppose the idea is to tear down one police state only to quickly erect another as soon as a bad virus hits our shores.

Tim Wise is a perfect example of the type I'm referring to. I take specific aim at this "antiracist activist," who, like many others, has made a nice income by raging against white America. But Wise is not only a racist; he's also a fascist. Having read a number of his books, listened to more than a few of his lectures, and following him on Twitter for a while, I have no doubt about this characterization.

Here is a man who harbors violent and intolerant tendencies, not unlike those Klan members he finds in every nook of society. He is every bit the authoritarian as the worst LA cop, and although we can't be sure he would ever put on a uniform, he would surely like to see you thrown in jail for the most minor of offenses, like refusing a vaccine or opening your place of business.

We already knew Wise's true colors, but the pandemic made them even brighter and more vibrant.

The criticism applies for others, like Radley Balko, whose excellent history of policing I make good use of. Balko, these days writing for the *Washington Post*, was completely silent about lockdowns and vaccine mandates. Indeed, he promoted vaccines and masking on his Twitter. If my (again unreliable) memory is correct, my questions on this matter led to me getting a block.

There oughta be a law against digital discrimination!

Both are big believers in white privilege and social impunity. But are they correct? Is there a disparity when it comes to abuses inflicted by the police? Or do the facts I cite get us closer to the truth? We live in an age of "infobesity." We search the internet, our source of constantly flowing facts, and find a study that proves something. Someone disputes it, and so finds another study that contradicts the first study.

Stack a pile.

Grab one and lob it like a grenade at your opponent. I hope no one gets that same impression here. Instead, I've cited a number of studies. The reader can make up their own mind. Numbers have never been my strength (blame my ADHD), so

I'm open to correction. But even without the studies, one cannot discount all the white people who've been killed by police. The most memorable incident was the homicidal beating of Kelly Thomas. I then go on to list, in parenthesis, almost thirty others. I urge readers to follow up with those names.

But how do we determine what deaths are tainted with racial animus?

Peering into the mind of another person is a very difficult thing to do. There could even be white cops who were once racist against blacks, but who later had a change of heart. They might've then wished for younger blacks to grow up in safer neighborhoods, thus giving them a reason every time they stuck their hands in someone's pocket.

Could be!

It's dogmatic to say that no white cop, in any part of the country, was ever motivated by that goal. Then again, maybe they're all Nazis.

Nevertheless, the ranks of America's law enforcement have its share of people of color.

According to Zippia, 12 percent of police are black, while 18 percent are Hispanic or Latino (whatever your designation is). So, did Mr. Ramos have racial intentions when he was murdering Kelly Thomas? I wonder the same about the officer who assaulted me all those years ago, as he was also Hispanic.

The question isn't unimportant, but it is secondary. The main concern is that America's law enforcement is running amok. There's more than a "few bad apples." And the "good apples" are either not interested, or too cowardly, to break through the Blue Line.

As with any argument or composition, there's always

something new to add.

Rereading this piece, I feel I should have included more criticism of those reliable defenders of the police: conservatives. Since were now post-pandemic, I can't figure out why conservatives remain so loyal to the authorities who made the lockdowns possible. Business owners, socialites, and churchgoers were routinely greeted by people with badges, resulting in many citizens getting fined or arrested simply for running afoul of the lockdown orders.

The question is then: Can the police ever do anything wrong? Or are they unassailable? If someone is killed, the "don't tread on me" folk like to assert: "they should have complied." If video footage shows the police beating a man on the sidewalk, the self-proclaimed Christians will forego both evidence and empathy and thus conclude that the cop must've been in the right.

I wonder if that holds true for victims of the lockdowns.

Furthermore, if a racial disparity does not exist, I don't use that fact as a way to offer unconditional support for the police. The Right seems to love making the same argument I do (they abuse white people too) before concluding that there's nothing to worry about.

But this is absurd.

If it's correct that the police violate the rights of everyone, it only buttresses the main point. Extrajudicial punishment is not a part of their mandate. Killing people, beating people, planting fake evidence on people, lying on reports—these are all violations of their oath.

Which is not to say that there are neither good cops nor criminal citizens. We seek balance and proportion, young grasshopper. We need evidence of what transpired. Alas, we also live in a time of boundless rage and instant expertise. Damn the internet all to hell!

In fact, there's only one sentence in this essay that I now fully repudiate. That's when I lend "credence to the comments made on social media." This is wrong, even if it's not obvious. The rage we see in the comments section does not always reflect voting patterns. If you check in on "Conservative Twitter," you'd think everyone was against abortion, even as abortion access is constantly reaffirmed in deep Red States.

If you to the Left side of Twitter, you'd think puberty blockers were about to be sold over the counter, even as we find that many Democrats are generally opposed to gender ideology. More, in the age of AI, when we see the "Dead Internet Theory" become a reality, it seems increasingly likely that a good deal of the traffic on the major platforms is phony. I keep that single sentence in here to show that—hey, I'm not a robot; I make mistakes.

Anyway, if Mr. Wise does a lot of digging, he might find out where this piece was originally published. The blog long ago went defunct. The owner of that blog was a libertarian with a white nationalist persuasion. ("You see! I knew he was a Nazi!") I won't say his name, simply because I hardly knew him, and he seems to have disappeared from the internet. I haven't seen him produce any content in years. His blog featured longform content, and he was kind enough to publish this single piece. Sometime later, I asked if I could publish it elsewhere. He gave the okay.

If one wants to hear some antiwhite hatred, all one has to do is turn on MSNBC, or go to a university. That's some pervasive white supremacy, isn't it? But if you want to hear another side, you have to go to these smaller outlets.

While everyone was saying "black lives matter," I was saying "civilian lives matter." Although the phrase shows up here and there on the internet, I have to believe I was one of the first to use it.

I tried to make it popular.

Did I succeed?

Well, it's a 10,000-word essay, so of course not. The only influencers making waves are producing video-audio content, which I'm so hesitant to do. If I could empower the police to do one thing, it would be to crack down on all these podcasters and social media "influencers" (that's a joke, of course). Indeed, it's the main reason I've decided to turn this old essay into a booklet. I prefer the posterity and precision of the printed word.

Note on the text.

I've always been a bit verbose. Signs of an amateur writer. Nowadays, I'm much more careful when making sentences. Back when I was thinking more about this, I had been reading through an "intersectionality reader." It was a chore to get through the text, and it was easy to notice how much wordier they were than even I (this doesn't include Wise, whose writing, although always angry and bitter, is usually clear). To insult these thinkers, I tried to emulate their style. Rereading the piece now, I realize that some of my paragraphs sounded goofy. And so, they were edited. A few sentences were taken out entirely.

The history of law enforcement is fascinating, as is the case for most good enemies. For this essay, I read about a half dozen books, and cited as I felt necessary. If this essay serves no other purpose, I hope it's a decent outline. Although I challenge the argument of biased police abuse, no where do I deny America's racist history.

In fact, I explicitly state that it's one filled with racism. Everyone who tries to say otherwise usually sounds foolish. If my stance on America's police has softened even slightly through the years, just know that I do not apologize for my harsh language found in these pages. Why? Police still wield a lot of power, and so they can handle nasty words.

They don't need to be worshipped.

The whole thing leaves me wondering whether I should do an update to this piece. There are several newer books on policing and incarceration which I would love to review. But unlike the SJW's, I also feel it's important to tackle other issues (*Why are so Many Robots White?* the headline reads) I have no expertise in anything.

I'm a very disturbed dilettante, a failed essayist, and a hopeless activist.

I make mistakes and do the best I can.

Alas, there's too many who can never be wrong.

—K. M. Patten

Civilian Lives Matter!

*As I listened to the fallout from these stirring events,
I wondered if this might be a moment when the media
would reform themselves and only print actual news;
for one thing, not all explosions of temper and so on
are attributable to race. It would be nice if the media
realized how dangerous they are when they begin to
falsify motives which, to be blunt, they have no
authority to do. If a black person is in any way in a
jam of any kind, it is because he is responding to
racism or if a white person goes berserk over anything
with anybody, racism drove him to do it. This is a
great, great red herring like some giant whale gliding
across the pages of police dockets.*
—Gore Vidal, *America the Great…Police State*

WHEN EXAMINING THE American citizenry, specifically
endowments and experiences that seem to be incognizable, one

discovers the most frustrating dilemma.

What should be easy enough to answer has become a vehicle for intransigence: What human lives, in this society, truly do matter?

Don't they all?

No, definitely not.

Though personally, the deeply-held convictions of my fellow countrymen have had me very perturbed (insert "white tears" comment here), and themselves coming largely from the black community, along with many employed at the White Guilt Industry, including updated nonsense given by members of the modern day feminist movement, and then any assortment of individuals conscripted via stealthy and unsolicited recruitment; taken together, they amount to a sizable lot who believe that I have some kind of immunity against state violence—indeed, am complicit in it—and this because of the neo-carnal sin of uncontrollable association with these Caucasian characteristics, and, furthermore, someone attached to a penis.

During their reading of that long last sentence, the "Critical Race Theorists," "Intersectionalist Movement," and so-called "Regressive Left" had a designation mentally reassured at least a dozen times: just another unthinking, guilt-soaked *White Man!*

But that could hardly be argued without subliminal recognition.

Instead, what I harbor is ever conscious *fear.* Almost

mutual at that, now. This of the American Police State. That the celebrants of casuistry can't comprehend or sympathize with it means to me that a new sort of Balkanism has finally seen fulfillment.

The "underprivileged" members of society, with the irreconcilability of their Hatred, now witness it come full circle, this in the form of two variants of nationalism—*white* and *civic*—who have both made themselves well known, but with balanced coverage of the second being replaced in favor of scorn for the first.

As a sample of my thesis, seek no further than "anti-racist" activist Tim Wise, who can usually be found doing his raging televangelist act—dishonestly written on his book blurbs as "education." ("God loves you, but he is angry" *does sound* something like:

> *Admit your privilege, because if you don't, it's bad for white folks too.*

Wise writes[i] of the "gigantic national inkblot" that "blinds so many to the way in which black folks often experience law enforcement," lamenting the "disturbing number of whites [that] manifest something of a repetitive motion—a reflex nearly as automatic as the one that leads so many people to fire their weapons at black men in the first place," and then to "defend the shooter, trash the dead with blatantly racist rhetoric and imagery, and to deny that the incident or one's own response to it had anything to do with race."

Here is Wise's crux:

> *The reflex to deny that there is anything racial about the lens through which we typically view law enforcement…*

—noting a few cases in which armed white suspects have been taken alive—and then gushingly stating that:

...to white America, in the main, police are the folks who help get our cats out of the tree, or who take us on ride-arounds to show us how gosh-darned exciting it is to be a cop.

We experience police most often as helpful, as protectors of our lives and property.

Gee golly, how purple.

Yet Wise has a point: plenty of whites, when seeing mass numbers of blacks rioting and looting and plundering, dismiss their actions with primitive racist terminology, sometimes complete with simian overtones.

Besides the militarization of America's police, these same people would also decline a discussion about internecine behavior that is similarly seen[ii] by individuals sharing the same shade. Rather, arguments would hover on the use of media propaganda to instigate and deceive and deflect; probably as well, indoctrinated victimologies that always compliment mass Groupthink.

There must be a pivot point somewhere.

Likely, the average white person will justify the additional police attention on black America by stating that this group commits far more street crimes. Because it's merely a fact that within this loosely knit national "community," black individuals commit about half of the total violent street crimes, making an unequal proportion when compared with the many more numbered white majority.

This is something that even Wise doesn't dispute:

> *So on the one hand it is true that the arrest rates for the most serious offenses—murder, rape, aggravated assault and robbery—do closely mirror the offending rates as reported by victims to the Bureau of Justice Statistics each year in the annual crime victimization surveys. There is no disputing that rates of offending in these categories are racially imbalanced, with African Americans committing these crimes at higher rates than whites.*

Poverty, he then says, is the source of the behavior.

Police State, American Style

Nonetheless, there's a legitimate complaint to be leveled at America's police forces.

Many fine books have come out that detail the dystopia referenced inadequately by Orwellian and Huxleyan clichés. Ergo, it's necessary to sketch a preliminary image of what Black Lives Matter activists are getting at, and what the police state documenters have to rebuke whenever people dismiss concerns and casually laud the men and women in blue.

The patriots who have taken up the cause of celebrating and preserving American freedoms should know that the Revolutionary War was fought largely because of the British

Crown's violation of the Castle Doctrine, holding that "a man's home is his castle."

These "writs of assistance" saw troops entering the homes of the colonists to check for smuggled and untaxed goods. John Adams credited these abuses as the seeds for revolution. Upon witnessing the reaction given to the failed legal challenge raised by James Otis Jr., Adams wrote:

> Then and there was the first scene of the first act of opposition to the arbitrary claims of Great Britain. Then and there, the child Independence was born.

Previously as well, the *Quartering Act of 1765* required the colonists to shelter and feed British troops. Consequently, the main fear of the Framers was the erector of a centrally-organized "standing army" that would be superimposed on the citizenry and their sacred "castles."

Radley Balko, the indispensable historian of the U.S. police state, sees the Third Amendment as "symbolic": "No Soldier shall, in time of peace be quartered in any house, without the consent of the Owner, nor in time of war, but in a manner to be prescribed by law." Only one major legal dispute has arisen over this Amendment.

And it sounds silly when considering that "standing armies" could simply build their own ramparts. But combined with the Second and Tenth, there was a bulwark against such tyranny.

Realism wins over idealism. Within the human mind

resides the want for control. More sadly, the impulse is tempered with impassive appeasement. American experimentation—liberty at last!—make the hypocrisies Three-Dimensional.

Civilian Lives Matter!

Historically, one observes a proverbial "tug of war" between local and federal power. A year after the ratification of the Bill of Rights, George Washington used the *1792 Calling Forth Act* to summon a militia to crush the Whiskey Rebellion taking place in Western Pennsylvania.

An answer to this incident was the *1807 Insurrection Act*, a series of laws intended to limit the use of the military in domestic affairs. Federal power could now only be used as a last resort, or when a state had directly asked for that assistance; to send the federal government in regardless of that request, there had to be a situation so dire that federal law could no longer be enforced, or that basic citizen rights were being violated with total negligence by their local governments.

Painfully, the issue of black enslavement, and the inevitable calls for a proper remedy, also helped to smudge, char, and snip away at the Castle Doctrine. For example, pre-Civil War, federal troops were bestowed the authority to capture and return runaway slaves. (As it is, the first police forces were "slave patrols.")

When the war concluded, those same federal troops were tasked with *protecting* the rights of newly-freed slaves. This was in place until the Compromise of 1877, which effectively ended Reconstruction. Then came the Progressive Era, which saw a new intelligentsia that dispelled the tenets of federalism and replacing them with an easy recognition for the need of a Leviathan state.

Launched thereabout was the War on Drugs, followed by

casualties consisting of both freedoms and lives. Alcohol was prohibited. When that project failed, cannabis became the focus. Journalist Johann Hari, profiling Drug War progenitor Harry Anslinger, the first Commissioner of the Federal Bureau of Narcotics, writes in his remarkable book *Chasing the Scream* that "prohibition had been abolished and his [Anslinger's] men needed a new role."

Originally, Anslinger had little quarrel with cannabis, thinking of it as distraction from the persecution of harder drugs. Why the change? Because he was a seething racist who came to realize (so he thought) that blacks and Mexican immigrants were using the plant to make white women promiscuous and decadent. (The Chinese, he charged, would use opium.) Anslinger, who enjoyed using the N-word to refer to his black agents, neglected the opinion of twenty-nine experts who said to ignore it and going with the single one who had demonized pot.

The Left has that truism correct: as with the very founding of the nation, the origins of the Drug War are drenched in a disgusting and vicious racism. Anslinger, a federal agent, then began prosecuting both black jazz musicians (the sound of which he thought came straight from hell), and doctors who were treating addicts with prescribed dosages. So much for State's Rights and decentralized power. Drug War update: in 2016, more people were arrested for cannabis-related activities than for anything else.[iii]

The component that accompanied the Castle Doctrine is—

was—the Exclusionary Rule, stating that any evidence obtained during an event in which a suspect's Constitutional rights had been violated cannot be admissible in a court of law. A century ago—year: 1914—the Supreme Court upheld the principle, this in *Weeks V. United States.* All presidents since have done their part to see that it would not last.

In the 1980's, under the approving eye of the "conservative" Reagan administration, the Castle Doctrine was decisively incinerated. It started with *U.S. V Leon*, wherein the Supreme Court found "good faith" in America's law enforcement: if an officer violates a suspect's Fourth Amendment, his intentions would not be probed, and the Exclusionary Rule tossed out the window. In *U.S. V Segura,* the Court ruled that police did nothing unconstitutional when they broke into a house and loitered around inside for nineteen hours, because they hadn't actually begun searching until a warrant was given.

In *Nix V. Williams*, the Court created the insidious doctrine of "inevitable discovery," stating that valid evidence could still be harvested from illegal searches, as the warrant would have been given anyway. "At this point," Balko opines in his book *Rise of the Warrior Cop*, "there wasn't really any real debate about policy. It was really only about which party could come up with the most creative ways to empower cops and prosecutors, strip suspects of rights, and show they were more committed to the battle than their opponents were."

This almost seems redundant; after all, it's estimated that

between 50-70 thousand "no-knock" police raids happen every single year, with most of them for mere execution of a warrant (cited from Whitehead).

In that same half-century, the federal government started supplying arms and money to local police departments. This began with the Johnson administration's creation of the Bureau of Narcotics and Dangerous Drugs (BNDD), which later became the DEA (Drug Enforcement Administration). The Supreme Court was also continuing to whittle away at the Castle Doctrine, specifically with *Terry V Ohio* (1968), ruling that "reasonable suspicion" was enough cause to stop people on the streets and interrogate them. From the Wikipedia entry:

> *Proper adjudication of cases in which the exclusionary rule is invoked demands a constant awareness of these limitations. The wholesale harassment by certain elements of the police community, of which minority groups, particularly Negroes, frequently complain, will not be stopped by the exclusion of any evidence from any criminal trial. Yet a rigid and unthinking application of the exclusionary rule, in futile protest against practices which it can never be effectively used to control, may exact a high toll in human injury and frustration of efforts to prevent crime.*

Another crime against American citizens is "civil asset forfeiture." Explicitly, the Constitution stipulates that property cannot be taken from anyone unless that person is convicted of a crime. "The genesis for this widespread system of abuse," writes Cheryl Chumley in her book *Police State USA,* "was the *Comprehensive Drug Abuse Prevention and Control Act of 1970*, which was enacted to fight the rising drug trafficking epidemic and gave federal authorities the power to forfeit properties in drug-related cases." In the early 80's, Senator Strom Thurmond introduced legislation to liberalize "asset seizure," reducing the standard of proof needed for confiscation to a mere "suspicion," while also eliminating the exemption of certain types of real estate.

On September 30, 1982, the crime bill overwhelmingly passed the Senate, 95-1. Oddly, President Reagan vetoed the bill, stating that "the war on crime and drugs does not need more bureaucracy in Washington." [iv]

Unforeseen senility?

We'll never know.

Anyway, two years later, Reagan signed the *Comprehensive Crime Control Act of 1984,* which gave the drug warriors all the power they wanted. In 2014, it was reported that theft-by-law enforcement had surpassed the amount of property taken by burglars, $5 billion to 3.5 billion. [v]

The complaints were so loud that by the late nineties, even the Clinton Administration—police state augmenters in their own right—had to sign legislative reform. Years later, now, the Supreme Court, as well as countless headlines, are sharing in this assessment. [vi]

Constitutional lawyer John Whitehead, in his book *A Government of Wolves*, has explored how this police state has evolved and adapted with every advancement in technology. Half of his wonderfully accessible report is a preview of the scariest and most sinister hardware to ever jump out of a work of fiction.

In 2009, the Los Angeles Police Department introduced a prototype "smart" police car, equipped with license plate cameras, computers, a GPS projection launcher, "and even a heat detector in the front grill to differentiate between people and animals." We find out that "police officers across the country" are using something called a Mobile Offender Recognition and Information System—or, MORIS.

Foreshadowing the iPhone X, this device first scans your face, which can include your irises, and then matches them against others already downloaded into government databases.

Databases! Edward Snowden risked everything to bring us the details of PRISM, the top-secret program that collects communications from all the top internet companies; IE, a flesh-and-bone God who watches everybody. Again, this policy isn't exactly new: the FBI has been spying on American dissidents for many decades, notably Martin Luther King Jr. "Big Data," the mass flow of information that's assumed to be inaccessible, made things easier for our rulers. Chumley writes:

> *Specifically, PRISM let the NSA (National Security Agency) collect users' search histories, email content, file transfers, and even live chats…*

Even James Comey admitted[vii] that "there's no such thing as absolute privacy in America.

In early 2016, it was reported that the Obama

Administration was going to relax restrictions on data-sharing, which per the ACLU,[viii] means that "domestic law enforcement officials now have access to huge troves of American communications, obtained without warrants, that they can use to put people in cages."

A few years earlier, *USA Today* reported[ix] that one-in-four departments used a tactic called "tower dump," giving them access to information contained on a person's phone.

The Electronic Envelope looks to be the final phase of any modern Police State, bringing us inside and around those black circles that pervade us, be it the tip of a gun or the lens of a camera.

"Not all cops" is the regular retort of police state apologists.

No, not all officers are violent.

But all officers are equipped with the instruments that *allows* for unchecked violence, much like how unnamed officials at the NSA can be *slightly* intrusive.

Heed the timeline: American Revolution is fought, a primary reason as for the defense of property. American constitution is signed, allows for the enslavement of human beings that are one day going to win their freedom and citizenship. Centralized powers are wielded to keep the bondages tight and secure. Citizens try, sometimes successfully and sometimes not, to wrest that power for their own purposes.

With the slave finally freed from his master (at least on paper), "ethical" brokers mosey their way onto the scene, seeking to forge new methods of control; of course, it's only meant to stop poison peddlers and to keep us safe from criminals and terrorists.

Today we witness modes of intrusion that, even sixty years ago, would've been inconceivable. The American Police State can tap your phones, search your pockets, raid your house, surveil your internet activity, and confiscate your property without a criminal conviction.

And it's all…*legal.*

Bastiat's explanation of how the State flips its function might now see a textbook case. It's enough to warrant the paranoia that flares up every time I meet a person working in law enforcement.

Interesting anecdote: I was once called a "cuck" for criticizing people in uniform. Sure, letting your country be overrun by cultures with different values and who feed from the public trough—that's the political, social, and economic equivalence of watching on humiliated as your wife gets ravaged by other men. (I can understand and sympathize with the implied argument.)

But cheerfully allowing some unelected, overpowered, overpaid officer to put his hands down your pants because you happened to be out walking near the crepuscular hour, or remaining unconcerned of that NSA agent who monitors your browsing habits while keeping track of your collection of sex toys—*right*, there's nothing "cucky" about this. Yes?

No.

So when trying to find common ground with all Americans, one ought to ignore those occasional (okay, more than occasional) up-close encounters with random bigotry and to spend that time instead discussing the conditions of life under this failed/rogue American state, with the focus on how to improve your own—insisted as *dire*—position in relation to this conclusively policed society.

Studying the situation as a liberty-eating entity that needs to be overcome, we can separately but simultaneously effect a collective attitude shift when viewing the current labor practices of the demented modern versions of Sheriff Taylor and Barney Fife.

We can then create treaties on things like acceptable

behavior and how to enforce these principles amongst our neighbors.

And since our subject is that violent institution of federalized law enforcement and acknowledging the history of abuse first visited upon black people in America, it's responsible to report that, compared to their counterparts, according to certain recent polls,[x] white America's support and trust for that rank-and-file is still relatively high.

But: am I the only who gives credence to the comments made on social media, and who notices a disdain that is *very often* shown by white people towards the kind of cops we're dealing with here?

Admitted to with a slightly unhealthy obsession: I keep my finger on that pulse, this mostly through Mr. Zuckerberg's network, that along with YouTube (Reddit is also popular) and do see those often-anonymous statements as vital evidence when trying to visualize a model of the polarized American mind.

If a 140-character Tweet is seen by the media as okay to quote, why forbade two other platforms which grant an extended space to expound?

We're not all robots yet!

Besides, if the aforementioned polls suggest that more than half of whites support the police, that still leaves some 30% or more that *might not* support them.

If one were to extrapolate this disinclination to two hundred thousand whites, it would not be insignificant, especially since the disparity is even greater with the younger generation.

Moreover, Pew inquired[xi] on the national thought of two high profile cases in which encounters with the police had led to the death of black men.

They found that Black America overwhelmingly saw the demise of Eric Garner, a New Yorker who was choked to death in July of 2014, as exactly the same as Michael Brown, who died the following month in Missouri; that the Grand Jury was wrong not to indict either of the officers, and, as insisted, that race was a major factor in both instances.

But when it came to White America, there was a sharp divide: only 28% expressed approval at the decision not to indict Garner's killer, with 47% believing that to have been wrongheaded.

However, they largely disagreed when it came to Brown, with 64% seeing the death as justified. Why? Because the facts are different: Brown was a young man whose last full act upon this earth was to commit a strong-arm robbery, and then— according to several reports—attacked one Officer Wilson, going for his gun, and eventually charging back at him after first running away.

Say what we will of American police forces (and I'll say enough), robbing a store and attacking a cop is not a scenario in which middle class white folks are going to sympathize with.

With Garner, all of America saw a man, accused only of selling "loose" cigarettes, pleading to be left alone, then being strangled to death on a suddenly emptied sidewalk.

How to tilt?

Polling data shows that white Americans are generally unhappy[xii] with the surveillance state, as they are about civil asset forfeiture[xiii]—even if they are unfortunately apathetic to the violence seen on city streets.

Cue the article telling us that whites only care about property. But if they are to be kicked awake, and made aware of the Police State, then the connection between the two should be attempted.

In the main: I do believe this to be a grotesque generalization of the sympathy felt for the victims of state intrusion, noting too that it's made by someone who makes his living by speaking out against the undue use of generalizing, but really not all that unexpected out of the mouth and fingers of America's foremost promotor of Separation.

Elaboration is forthcoming.

Racial Obscurantism

Returning to *incognizable endowments and experiences*—the "anti-racist" perception that insists a kind of impunity based on whiteness, and rather a permanent target placed on the backs of black people—we can see that this mindset has seeped into the larger institutional framework, as demonstrated by the "elite" Bank Street School for Children on the Upper West Side, which has a curriculum that teaches white children that they are born racists.[xiv]

The "educators" then separate black kids from white to raise "awareness of the prevalence of Whiteness and privilege," so reports the *NY Post*.

A FAQ put out by the school addresses the obvious: Is this a form of segregation?

No, they say, segregation is a government policy that

benefits one group over the other; this is a program meant to address "the sociological and psychological needs of children of color in a predominately white setting."

If they're upset about the amount of white people, one might ask, why not attend a school devoted entirely to black people?

Those really exist! And they aren't deemed racist.

An individual example of an "educator" absolutely awash in their pathological self-hatred is one Ali Michael, an Ivy League professor at the University of Pennsylvania, who wrote an essay for *The Huffington Post* explaining why she can't bring herself to biologically procreate.[xv]

She writes:

> *If I was going to pass on my privilege, I wanted to pass it on to someone who doesn't have racial privilege; so I planned to adopt. I disliked my Whiteness, but I disliked the Whiteness of other White people more.*

And we know how serious she is because of the amount of times she uses the capitalized word "Whiteness."

Michael finishes with saying:

> *But we cannot not be White. And we cannot undo what Whiteness has done. We can only start from where we are and who we are.*

One almost gets the sense that if this person ever did have offspring who were white, and if those children were one day assaulted on the playground by a child of another race, there would be a quick masochistic sigh of relief, indicating that generational justice had finally come to pass.

Verily, it's good that she abstains from giving birth to such a creature, lest she ever consider the Chris Benoit contingency.

Despite Wise thinking it's his side that has the intellectual grit, it's in fact Intersectionalism that's hooked up with the unhinged.

Dangling insanely is an Occupy veteran, one Alissa Kokkins, who helped organize the "hands up" protests in LA, and writing this for The Anti-Media:

> *I am still critiquing and deconstructing my own position on playing the roll* [its spelled role, but then we all make those minor grammatical errors] *of organizer. Especially, since I, like many white people there, put my hands up and chanted: 'Hands Up! Don't shoot!' Ignoring a quiet voice in my head that said, 'White people should be screaming 'hands up', while people of color put their hands up and chant back 'don't shoot'.*

How utterly inclusive and nonjudgmental, just as the Occupy movement was intended!

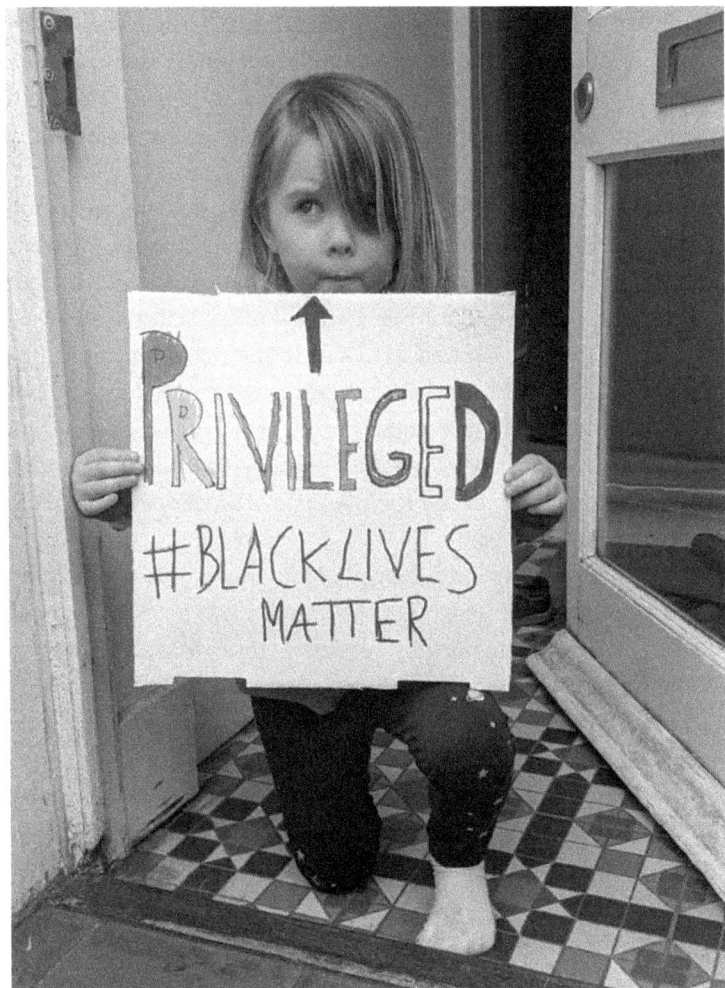

From here, these strange accusations of authority become even more invidious, as in that very popular blog post that appeared on a page called ManicPixieDreamMama.com, and was again prototypically mistitled, *A White Mother's Privilege* (picked up by HuffPost).[xvi]

These activists often—and sometimes do—mean to say *Power*, ignoring the natural separation one *should have* with every so-called justice department—not to forget Washington, Wall Street, and of course their international officials in the CIA.

As with other stunted letters from the absurdist ambit, this imaginatively loathsome piece, saturated with emotion and totally devoid of any substance or study whatsoever, has but one silly conclusion: all persons of a lighter pigmentation are born into a world that inculcates their brains with a desire to kill black people.

Generating several hundred comments worth of gratitude (I am positive that at one point the number was hovering around 1,400), many from persons of color, though with plenty of pathetically guilt-ridden white people as well, it said, to wit: "I'm so *very* worried that my kid might grow up and kill your kid."

Creating a synopsis of this ridiculousness (great parenting by the way: "Have a nice day son, please remember not to murder anybody"), an extraction of several sentences ran consecutively:

To admit white privilege is to admit a stake, however

small, in ongoing injustice…Acknowledging that your own group enjoys social and economic benefits of systemic racism is frightening and uncomfortable…I have three sons, two years between each. They are various shades of blond, various shades of pinkish-white, and will probably end up dressing in polo shirts and button downs most of the time. Their eyes are blue and green. **Basically, I'm raising the physical embodiment of The Man, times three. The White is strong in these ones**…*Clerks do not follow my sons around the store, presuming they might steal something…People do not assume that, with three children, I am scheming to cheat the welfare system…***I will not worry that the police will shoot them**…*For a mother, white privilege means your heart doesn't hit your throat when your kids walk out the door…It carries another burden instead. White privilege means that if you don't school your sons about it, if you don't insist on its reality and call out oppression, your sons may become something terrifying.* **Your sons may become the shooters***.
[Emphasis added]

The personal story of this blond-haired, hazel-eyed male, absolved of any such racial murder and someone who has no stupid prognostications for his own whitely (though mixed) son? Only briefly. In these United States, in my ripening early thirties, and according to recently disclosed court reports, I have been arrested *sixteen times* (a few drunk-in-public accounts appear to have gone missing), starting with a petty theft at age fifteen; with booze, I thought innumerably; same with driving like a madman; and even spending three years in prison for an immature and bizarre (embarrassing and pitiful) form of terrorism (which I won't get into), with some four arrests post-release (so much for "criming while white"). Obvious disclaimer: depending on the narrative being pushed, anecdotes can be important to some people at certain times, and unimportant at other times.

As I attempted to articulate in one of my "police state" essays, these experiences should not serve as badges or "brownie points." Prison and jail stints *ought not* (save for this ironic paragraph) be notches in one's belt. Instead, remorseful separations, a man (or woman) away from his (or her) Time & Freedom. Many (*many*) adapt. *Some* learn. Others, nigh.

And thankfully, I don't currently live in any such dungeon. I breathe fresh(er?) air. And as intimated, I love being able to experience maniacal motoring, the full gust of going 10 or 15 miles (all arbitrary numbers, just as the police demonstrate when racing to the scene of a crime at 100 MPH) over the speed limit while the scenery quickly disappears from behind.

Freedom enough.

But I also hate it: always with the possible tyranny—or should I say *intrusive assault*? Even when there aren't any black-and-white cars in my rearview, the eye always catches a possibility of them: two vehicles—one dark, one light—

contrasting at the intersection.

Afraid upon a confirmed sighting of one of these bacon-mobiles (I mean police cars!), I typically turn down another street in an effort to evade the initiation of any criminal infraction (seatbelts can be so uncomfortable). I've been hoofed in the head by a pig (I mean respectable upholder of the Law!), once. Twice had guns fixed upon me. Continuously cursed at. Threatened with legal kidnapping. Placed in the back of a bacon-mobile while my own bohemian-mobile was ransacked. And yes: "stopped and frisked" at least several dozen times in this dreadful LA Valley (I loathe just about all of Los Angeles), and usually for nothing more than walking down the street after the hour of the undeclared curfew at nine 'o clock.

So, when black bystanders tell white cameramen in New York City that they're lucky to be of that shade[xvii] (notice the color of this threatening oinker), or else they would have already been in cuffs, I can't act as goofily[xviii] (seriously, what's wrong with some of these psychotics?) as a white "Intersectionalist" will, annoyingly insistent that the pronouncement is correct.

As far as what other *white folks* (Wise's *Kumbaya* terminology, which I've been wanting to type) might say about this idea of inherited protection against police abuse (or was that Power and its usage?), one could ask the family of Kelly Thomas. Or Samantha Ramsey. Or Charles Eimers. Or Zack Hammond. (Or: Douglas Zerby, Autumn Steele, Robert Ethan Saylor, Betty Sexton, Gilbert Collar, Nick Christie, Danielle

Maudsley, Dillon Taylor, Keith Vidal, Jeanetta Marie Riley, Edward Miller, Robert Cameron Redus, Eugene Mallory, David Dehmann, David Kassick, Jack Yantis, Robert Earl Lawrence, Danielle Willard, Ronald Hillstrom, Tyler Comstock, James Boyd, John Wrana, Christopher Roupe, John Livingston, Ryan Keith Bolinger, Raymond Keith Martinez…just in case Wise and the Talking-Heads forgot to mention some of them.)

Civilian Lives Matter!

Those unnecessary casualties lay alongside many more, darker-skinned corpses. Among the most tragic, Rumain Brisbon, gunned down while coming home to feed his children; Tamir Rice, also shot, this time for wielding a toy gun; Philando Castile, killed during a traffic stop in which a Hispanic officer thought he had found suspected robbers, who then got scared when finding out about Castile's legally possessed firearm, quickly putting four bullets in him; Eric Garner, just discussed; and, the most tearful on this list, seven-year old Aiyana Jones, murdered by a trigger happy police officer amid a botched (as many such intrusions are) Chicago-evening raid.

The abuse of power by the police in this country has become so noticeable that even the United Nations[xix] has condemned it, and indeed specifying minority populations as the primary victims.

Though I would more like to agree with John Vibes,[xx] a researcher working at that useful police abuse database, The Freethought Project, who said about the psychology of these government forces:

> *In many ways, this mentality has justified the unjustifiable abuse, harassment and murder of countless people, from all different races and ethnic backgrounds. Being different isn't a crime, but it does seem to make you an outlaw.*

Different? We can all hate the State.

Numbers? The data for police killings is notoriously incomplete. This is mainly because the studies are based on "self-reporting"—and, as a rule, police officers cannot lie. As exampled above, unaccountable officers *can* and *do* exercise lethal force against everyday Americans. According to *Mother Jones*,[xxi]

> *The Justice Department's Bureau of Justice Statistics reports that between 2003 and 2009 there were more than 2,900 arrest-related deaths involving law enforcement. Averaged over seven years, that's about 420 deaths a year. While BJS does not provide the annual number of arrest-related deaths by race or ethnicity, a rough calculation based on its data shows that black people were about four times as likely to die in custody or while being arrested than whites.*

The liberal journal then adds:

> *The CDC's cause-of-death data, based on death certificates collected at the state level, also reveals a profound racial disparity among the victims of police shootings. Between 1968 and 2011, black people were between two to eight times more likely to die at the hands of law enforcement than whites. Annually, over those 40 years, a black person was on average 4.2 times as likely to get shot and killed by a cop than a white person. The*

> *disparity dropped to 2-to-1 between 2003 and 2009,*
> *lower than the 4-to-1 disparity shown in the BJS data*
> *over those same years.*

In April of 2015, the conservative-leaning Washington Times[xxii] reported on an analysis done by Peter Moskos, assistant professor at the John Jay College of Criminal Justice, who looked at data from the website KilledByPolice.net. What he found was that:

> *49 percent of those killed by officers from May 2013 to*
> *April 2015 were white, while 30 percent were black…*

also finding…

> *…that 19 percent were Hispanic and 2 percent were*
> *Asian and other races.*

PolitiFact confirms this:

> *Over the span of more than a decade, 2,151 whites died*
> *by being shot by police compared to 1,130 blacks.* [xxiii]

Black America is only 13% of the population, but, as Paul Joseph Watson concludes, "they are *underrepresented* if you factor in violent crime offenders. In other words," the infowarrior reports, "you would expect the number of blacks and whites killed by police to be roughly equal given that they commit a roughly equal number of violent crimes, but that's not the case. Whites are nearly 100% more likely to be victims."

A professor of economics at Harvard, one Roland Fryer,[xxiv] made media waves in the Summer of 2016 after releasing a study on police violence. Fryer had looked at police shootings in ten major departments. Utilizing four different sets of data—"none ideal" (due mainly to the reliance on officer reporting)—and containing "roughly" five million observations, Fryer's paper, not peer-viewed, had many startling findings. When it came to mere physical contact with the police, there were "large racial differences" between those involving whites and that of blacks and Hispanics. The latter are fifty percent "more likely to have an interaction with the police which involves any use of force." A "small number" of stops (as in stopping and frisking) result in the discovery of illegal contraband, some 3 percent.

However, when it came to interactions with the police that resulted in fatalistic outcomes, Fryer found that blacks are "23.8 percent *less* likely to be shot by police, relative to whites. Hispanics are 8.5 percent less likely to be shot but the coefficient is statistically insignificant." Fryer concludes: "We cannot detect racial differences in officer-involved shootings on any dimension." How 'bout that? A black Harvard economist has confirmed that they *do* kill white people!

It's not surprising that during an interview[xxv] with Chauncey DeVega, Wise—that shill for the Deep State, what with his "nonchalance" about the revelations revealed bravely by

Civilian Lives Matter!

Edward Snowden and Glenn Greenwald (again, to hell with American citizens—because those are mainly white males, "people who have never before been presumed criminal, up to no good, or worthy of suspicion.")—not only lambasted Fryer's research, he dismissed the professor entirely as a "radical centrist…black centrist."

In effect: How *dare* Fryer investigate the casualty rates of *all people* at the hands of American law enforcement! It is always racial hatred that singles out "black 'n brown folks" (one and the same, of course)—and that's the end of it.

What is the intimidating "radical black centrist"?

Wise, who is far more insightful and moralistic than these types, kindly leaves a clue. Earlier on the show, Wise deploys an awe-inspiring *reductio ad absurdum* when "debunking" the argument that some of White America's support for Donald Trump was truly because they had accepted his promise to bring back their jobs. This consideration is beyond Wise. Every motivation of white people, the bearers of absolute power, must be due to "I don't like 'dem niggers 'n wetbacks." "If it were otherwise," Wise says, "he would also have had support from black folks." But as he knows—because he's a smart guy—Trump, who spoke a lot about creating jobs for black youth, got more black votes than Mitt Romney did.[xxvi]

Of course, Black America still primarily votes Democratic. Perhaps there'd be more black conservatives—and hopefully a lot more "centrists"—if Wise stopped dismissing every black thinker who doesn't share his thoughtful and nuanced (cease sarcasm!) worldview as "working for the man."

Like plenty of others, Mr. Wise is obsessed with whiteness to the point that he's willing to blame any human problem on the white male, while ignoring or downplaying other groups that should also be charged with moral and political criminality. (We're not talking about what's written on paper).

And he often acts childishly: on Twitter, Wise opines that Snowden and Greenwald—no heroes, according to him—will not be the ones to bring down the American Empire; then, snippily responding to someone, adds "nor will you."

But I'm sure that Wise—"they must be destroyed completely!"—has a different opinion of his own efforts.

Or, maybe he's getting paid enough not to care either way.

After all, Wise has the...*privilege*...to go back to his affluent all-white neighborhood in Tennessee, where he sits and reads and thinks of clever jabs he can take at White America; at the beckon of a suitable headline, he springs up so as to bark at the mythical tribe of malefactors, who are apparently ignorant of their participation in every act of wrongdoing that's known to everyone else in the world.

By the way, there's nothing wrong with living in wealthy homogenous areas—except for someone who makes a living by seeing *everything* in terms of white oppression.

This is someone who has written:

> *I swear, if I hear one more transparently racist person insist they aren't racist because they have black friends, I am going to shoot them.*

What was that about the "climate of hate"?

It's hard to imagine this blowhard convincing anyone of anything.

Therefore, I see him as an advocate for separation, as it must dawn on him that he only galvanizes the populace and emboldens white nationalists whenever they hear his brand of stupidity.

Who is "We" and What Can They Do?

Seems that I have digressed. There are a few more studies worth looking at, one of which counters the work of Professor Fryer. In 2015, Professor Cody Ross at UC Davis authored *A Multi-Level Bayesian Analysis of Racial Bias in Police Shootings.* [xxvii]

He found that there's a "significant bias in the killing of unarmed black Americans relative to unarmed white Americans, in that the probability of being (black, unarmed, and shot by police) is about 3.49 times the probability of being (white, unarmed, and shot by police) on average."

Ross, too, acknowledges the inadequacy of the data. And contradictory as the data is, I cite it for the sake of the roundest discussion we can generate.

The work of Michelle Alexander is often granted as a standard thesis, almost self-explanatory in the title of her book, *The New Jim Crow*. Alexander compiles a great deal of information to prove that there is a "war" against black people. Some of this is very valuable to freedom fighters, like her discussion of Reagan's "Operation Pipeline," which trained officers to use traffic stops as a means for drug interdiction: lengthening the time of the stop, how to get reluctant drivers to consent to a search, and the use of drug-sniffing dogs.

Alexander also points out that, despite a Supreme Court ruling made forty years ago (*Gideon V Wainwright*) stating that impoverished criminal suspects still deserve legal counsel, "thousands" of people go through the court system every year without the aid of a lawyer, or with one who doesn't have the time or resources to properly defend them. In Wisconsin alone, "more than 11,000" poor suspects go to court without representation, the reason given because anyone who makes more than $3,000 a year is not considered "poor."

But then Alexander makes a claim that has recently been

countered, this in her introduction:

> *The impact of the drug war has been astounding. In less than thirty years, the U.S. penal population exploded from 300,000 to more than 2 million, with drug convictions accounting for the majority of the increase.*

My penultimate paragraph in this report will reference the contrary evidence. Criticism of the American Police State remains. The journal *Injury Prevention* did a study in which they found that American police killed or injured more than 55,000 in 2012, this due mainly to traffic stops and Stop & Frisk policies.[xxviii]

Again, minority groups were more likely to be the victims. One last one. According to a 2014 study by *Crime and Delinquency*, nearly half of black Americans are arrested before the age of twenty-three. Odd thing: it was the same for 40% of whites.[xxix]

No, it's still not an equal proportion—but it's quite a lot for everyone, contrary to what Comrade Sanders would have you believe.

Therefore, I can now create my own "hashtag": *Civilian Lives Matter!* "Civilian" is chosen specifically because it means "non-military," as our police forces have largely become.

I can already hear the howls: *You're a white man; you can't experience oppression!* Of course, until more rigorous documentation is made, it won't be possible to know exactly how many people die annually at the hands of law enforcement. In the meantime, to help keep track of police killings (without saying that all are unjustified), I urge everyone to check out *The Guardian's* indispensable new project, "The Counted."

Reasons! A theory of American policing requires at least

four animating factors and one rebuttal that's now been argued to its completion: the insurance of political and economic survival, mainly by persecuting the most vulnerable; a means to suppress revolutionary activism; to therapeutically remedy psychotic behavior via directing random violence towards innocent citizens; and the aggrandizement of state power stemming from participation in this so-called "democracy."

A thorough report would also debunk the simplistic assertion that "white supremacy" aims to eradicate non-whites, as the System still likes voters to exploit for their own purposes.

Following the last two items in the above paragraph, this underproduced inquiry: is there *any* responsibility to be given to Black America for this militarized atmosphere?

My assessment says yes, a small amount given electorally.

Malcolm X, in his autobiography, said that "well-meaning white people...had to combat actively and directly, the racism in white people."

For us troubled about the wellbeing of our fellow countrymen, as well as the history of the police state that enshrouds us all—good! Still, let's not hate our own children. The revolutionary leader then added that, "black people had to build within themselves much greater awareness that *along with equal rights there had to be bearing of equal responsibilities*." [Emphasis mine] Remember this was said during the time of the Voting Rights Act.

Malcolm believed that black people, if granted political enfranchisement, would have enough power to effectuate liberation.

Where did that route take us? Black America is a fairly "democratic" group, going to the booths at least every four years. A Census Bureau study conducted after the 2012 presidential election showed that, for the first time ever, blacks outvoted whites, 66% of eligible voters to 64%.[xxx]

Insofar as American Imperialism and the continued execution of the Drug War is concerned, those cast ballots have helped to elect politicians who've done some harm: Charles Rangel, Bill Clinton, Barack Obama, and—*almost!*—the Mrs. Clinton. Demonstrably, "institutional power" is wielded by other sectors of the population.

As for viable solutions, I once sought some from Kelly Thomas' father, Ron, himself a retired police officer who once gave online criticism of Michael Brown, which should lead to the final part of this discussion: agreeable appraisals (not whiny, indeed downright phony, emotional outbursts) that can be shared between both black *and* white America.

For starters, how to have the most effective people who're assigned the job of protecting life and property while also making them accountable to the people they serve?

This is tricky, but here I can be a true anarchist, with three basic proposals. 1.) Overturn, or annul, every Supreme Court ruling regarding law enforcement, starting with *Terry V. Ohio*. 2.) Start firing more police officers, aside from homicide detectives and—for the minute—prison guards. And 3.) Thereafter, make every police officer subject to a jurisdictional election and followed by an annual review.

Underlining what other commentators have suggested: police need to become *reactive* as opposed to *proactive*, making them comparable to firefighters.

Radical?

I would think so. Intentionally, these measures would strip the federal government of its authority. It won't be perfect, as localities might still want to crack down on drug users, but a blueprint for reform needs to start somewhere.

It cannot be argued that Black America has had it easy in America, particularly when confronted with the sharp edge of the State.

They felt it initially, and brutally. The Black Lives Matter movement, then, can be commended for bringing greater awareness to the American Police State. If it does this for both civilians and for law enforcement—if the former decides to look at it more objectively, while the latter comes to discern their immediate actions more closely—then that's a victory.

In the future, gullible Americans will no longer find themselves sliding down that stupid slope, conflating the reportage of a rape with that of a SWAT Team busting down the door. The line goes something like: *If you don't obey the command of every officer you ever encounter, then you should never call them for help.*

I might dare someone to look into the eyes of brave nurse Wubbels or college student Charnesia Corley and tell them the same thing.

Yet the movement is not without a few blemishes. It's my feeling that BLM has been made intolerable for two primary reasons. The first is this: when that anger becomes animated, it is usually directed, not at state actors or those who do the killing and the arresting, but rather those who are trying to get to work or go about their day-to-day activities. Regular cars are set ablaze; the police stations are left unscathed. Numerous videos show protesters blocking roads, preventing even ambulances from getting through. These tactics are likely to generate, not sympathy for the cause, but instead more calls for police vivacity.

Meanwhile, neighborhoods get looted and lit up. Some national publications sought to justify the destruction as invoked by someone (Yes, Mr. Wise) per MLK's assertion that a "riot is the language of the unheard." In that same clip, MLK hoped for a "vigorous protest" which was "non-violent," because "riots were self-defeating and socially destructive"—a sentiment he seemed to repeat many times. Still, he wanted the participants to be "militant and determined"—whatever that might mean to 21st Century ears. (I admit to not being too familiar with King's writings.) As Murray Rothbard wrote in his evaluation of "The Negro Revolution" (1963), "for mass invasion of private restaurants, or mass blocking of street entrances is, in the deepest sense, *also* violence."

In the aftermath of these highly publicized accounts, we can see a seismic rupture within the legal system; a disrespect no longer abstruse. Brown, a burglar and assailant, was suddenly and thoughtlessly made, as the default, into a martyr. (As already noted, black and white America had vastly different perspectives on the case.) But since Brown's death was a result of his own doing, as realized by any rational person, we ought to then interpret his actions, and those of his mourners, as something much more meaningful. I mean to say that Brown should be given some credit here: he first robbed a store, justly causing a police response, and then proceeded to attack the officer who did that, even briefly acquiring his gun.

By concluding that this was an innocent young man who did not need to die, deeming those who dared to mention his crimes as mere "racists" or "Uncle Toms," one must grant that, instead, he was an agent for a greater cause. "We are all Michael Brown"—said many black people. But why would anybody want to be that guy? A guess: he proclaimed, loudly, *"Fuck the white man's laws!"* Where his hands were at in the final few moments will matter very little, neither to civilized people who can conceive of some sort of communal security force, or to the eternally discontented who have a preferred interest in the "eradication" of White Supremacy.

If his flaunting of the law and the rights of private property (it was a supermarket he robbed) are to be excused, Brown ought to be given a proper mantle—perhaps akin to George Washington or Thomas Jefferson. His tombstone should read: *"White cops, white businesses, and white people—get out of the Black Community!"* He was a visionary separatist, although he never even knew it. This exertion thus helped spread, inadvertently, a sort of neo-separatism. Will it allow us to reconsider Malcolm X's dream of a separate nation within the nation?

Expounding on this. Ostensibly, social justice activists lament an oncoming apartheid. But when will they realize that, contra Mr. Wise, some of us *don't give a damn* about "multicultural democracy"? There are many who realize that certain forms of collectivism are—for now—inevitable, and that it's okay if people want to discriminate when it comes to those who they live and work and learn amongst. I don't think people like Mr. Wise want to admit to the general public just how truly divided it is.

Emphatically, homogeneity does not have a definition that entails only the matters of skin color (and pluralism has worked decently in some parts) but also more tangible differences based on language, culture, and religion: items that lead to inevitable division. The nationalists are correct: tensions often rise when perceptions are not shared universally. Even if the variables are hard to calculate, the human organism does seem to gravitate to those who share certain similarities, not all of them easy to do away with.

Needed for those who accept my theory of Brown-as-Revolutionary is a demarcation across geographical lines. This could finally see a true "black community." Federalism could also be restored, with independent states and communities making general agreements on trade. California might be our first experiment. If they succeed with secession, and afterwards abrogate federal law, then that's better than the rest of America, who will still be stuck with it (maybe California can set a good example!)

In short, there's a mishmash of both thoughtful and unthoughtful solutions, which creates confusion, and people should start a dispassionate project of unraveling them. "Not my job to educate you" is as hard on the ears as "why don't they just get over it?"

There's one last issue I have with the Black Lives Matter movement, already stated.

The spectrum of black liberation theology has widened, noticeably, finding itself into the deranged corners of postmodernism. In other words, the activism has become congenital to the academically ordained incoherence called "Intersectionality." Without exaggerating the nonargument, it's taken as truth that everyone who isn't a Straight White Male is an inmate that will eventually find themselves shackled-up vertically next to other inmates on the same prison block.

Deductively, homosexuals and immigrants and Muslims and women—both with and without penis—are all seen as participants on the same team, fighting against the same Oppressor.

The "intersection of oppression," or something like this. If there's any anti-blackness in Hispanic communities, it must be a conspiracy perpetrated by the White Man; nothing within the culture itself. Homophobia in black communities? Well, California's successful passing of Proposition 8, which (temporarily) banned gay marriage, must've required an army of homophobic white ninjas who forced those 70% of black voters to come out to the polls.

The sexist, transphobic, patriarchal nature of anybody else? Don't bother! Under this "theory," giving puberty blockers to a mentally disturbed 10-year-old can be viewed as the same "struggle" as that of Muslims in Dearborn who wish to mutilate the genitals of their female children (it is argued to be a First Amendment liberty, now a legally protected right of practicing members of the world's largest deathcult, Islam).

Adjusting for the myopia, it should be realized that all groups have been violent, bigoted, superstitious, and warlike, and that many in human history have also wielded Power, still trying to do that very thing. Let's beckon for both civility and sanity as we venture into utopia.

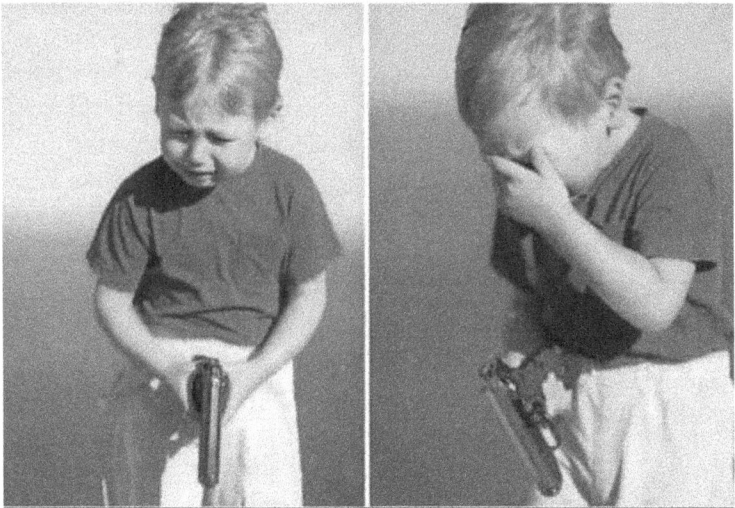

When you're a cop and your girlfriend asks you to do her doggy style

What will block that prospect? One can often hear rumblings of a coming "race war." Should we expect more confrontational events?

Here Wise makes an acute observation.

In his memoir, he recalls a time in which he answered this question to an "old white person" who had asked the same:

> *Actually, I said, we're already in a race war. It started several hundred years ago when white folks decided to exterminate Native Americans, and then continued when whites opted for the importation of slaves from Africa, ripping people from their homes, their cultures, their religions, their continent and bringing them to the land we were now on, so as to make Europeans wealthier.*

Per Mr. Wise, we've been at war. Who's on the frontlines? Cops? Rioters? Voters? At least I have my sword and shield made from whiteness. Henceforth, whenever I am accosted by a member of law enforcement, I should claim to be on the same team, and thus be on my way.

I can't wait to test my white privilege.

Or was it *power*?

There is another angle, one that I'll scratch my back on later. Professor John Pfaff at Fordham has been the subject of many articles as of late. His research shows that the problem of mass incarceration in America is hardly due to non-violent drug arrests. The presumption is correct only at the federal level, where roughly half of the 95,000 prisoners are there for drug crimes. When aggregating state prison populations, those same illegalities account for a mere 16 percent (still too many!). America is violent, even if the fingers are being pointed from every direction; and maybe violence begets violence. This would disrupt the narrative offered so candidly by civil libertarians.

Nevertheless, Americans—*all of them*—are overly-policed. Badge-holders driving the beat, and surveillance nerds who monitor screens, both wield an enormous amount of authority—one could even use the word *omnipresence*. It's not just about incarceration, but also the loss of liberty, theft of property, and all the many random acts of violence and corruption.

These violations have crept up slowly and silently, where they are now a function and not a defect. Too frequently, slime peddlers come out from under their rocks to rage furiously, perhaps cash a paycheck, and receive some street therapy.

Therefore, if we want an end to the abuse, we require a more civilized discussion on all matters that involve not only policing but also a culture that seeks to render objectivity itself as an annoying twitch in a doomed society full of never-ending power dynamics.

References

[i] https://www.alternet.org/2014/11/most-white-people-america-are-completely-oblivious

[ii] https://www.alternet.org/2014/11/11-stupid-reasons-white-people-have-rioted

[iii] https://www.nytimes.com/2016/10/13/us/marijuana-arrests.html

[iv]

https://www.washingtonpost.com/archive/politics/1983/01/15/objection-to-drug-czar-post/22db81ae-bc97-48e3-9da5-7a48bf5fcc3b/

[v]

https://www.washingtonpost.com/news/wonk/wp/2015/11/23/cops-took-more-stuff-from-people-than-burglars-did-last-year/

[vi] https://slate.com/news-and-politics/2017/04/the-supreme-court-justices-finally-found-an-issue-that-unites-them.html

[vii] https://www.cnn.com/2017/03/08/politics/james-comey-privacy-cybersecurity/index.html

[viii] https://www.washingtonpost.com/news/the-watch/wp/2016/03/10/surprise-nsa-data-will-soon-routinely-be-used-for-domestic-policing-that-has-nothing-to-do-with-terrorism/

[ix]

https://www.usatoday.com/story/news/nation/2013/12/08/cell-phone-data-spying-nsa-police/3902809/

[x] https://www.pewresearch.org/short-reads/2015/04/28/blacks-whites-police/

[xi] https://www.pewresearch.org/politics/2014/12/08/sharp-racial-divisions-in-reactions-to-brown-garner-decisions/

[xii] https://www.pewresearch.org/short-reads/2015/05/29/what-americans-think-about-nsa-surveillance-national-security-and-privacy/

[xiii] https://www.cato.org/blog/84-americans-oppose-civil-asset-forfeiture

[xiv] https://nypost.com/2016/07/01/elite-k-8-school-teaches-white-students-theyre-born-racist/

[xv] https://www.huffpost.com/entry/i-sometimes-dont-want-to-be-white-either_b_7595852

[xvi] https://www.huffpost.com/entry/a-mothers-white-privilege_b_5698263

[xvii] https://thefreethoughtproject.com/cop-watch/power-tripping-nypd-cop-tells-man-your-amendment-ends-here

[xviii] https://www.youtube.com/watch?v=J2paiKp6_YU

[xix] https://www.usatoday.com/story/news/world/2015/05/11/concerns-excessive-force/27107533/

[xx] https://thefreethoughtproject.com/the-state/police-cultural-profiling-target-free-thinkers-races

[xxi] https://www.motherjones.com/politics/2014/09/police-shootings-ferguson-race-data/

[xxii] https://www.washingtontimes.com/news/2015/apr/21/police-kill-more-whites-than-blacks-but-minority-d/

[xxiii] https://www.politifact.com/factchecks/2014/aug/21/michael-medved/talk-show-host-police-kill-more-whites-blacks/

[xxiv] https://www.youtube.com/watch?v=iwAK9qbOrAg

[xxv] https://www.youtube.com/watch?v=doisuCOxvAY
[xxvi] https://www.washingtonpost.com/news/monkey-cage/wp/2016/11/11/trump-got-more-votes-from-people-of-color-than-romney-did-heres-the-data/
[xxvii]
https://journals.plos.org/plosone/article?id=10.1371/journal.pone.0141854
[xxviii] https://www.independent.co.uk/news/world/americas/us-police-killed-or-injured-more-than-55-000-people-in-one-year-a7157321.html
[xxix]
https://www.usatoday.com/story/news/nation/2014/01/20/nearly-half-arrested/4669225/
[xxx] https://www.census.gov/newsroom/archives/2013-pr/cb13-84.html